the guide to owning a
Discus

W9-BAJ-546

Mary E. Sweeney

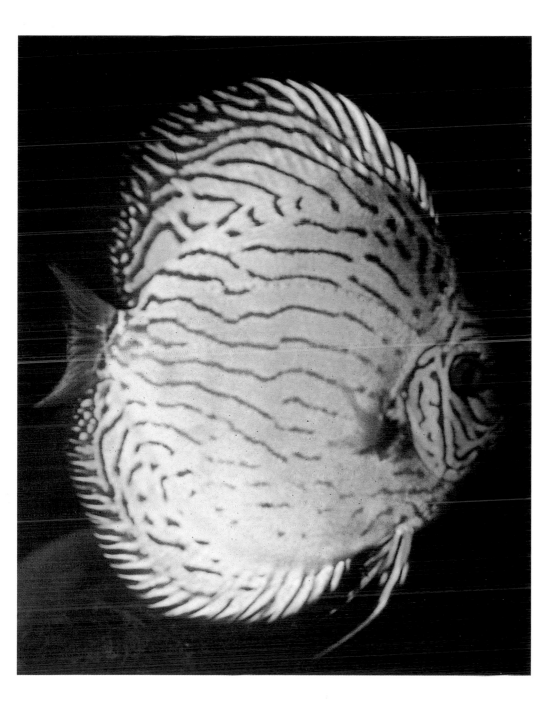

T.F.H. Publications, Inc.
One TFH Plaza
Third and Union Avenues
Neptune City, NJ 07753

This book has been published with the intent to provide accurate and authoritative information in regard to the subject matter within. While every precaution has been taken in preparation of this book, the publisher and author assume no responsibility for errors or omissions. Neither is any liability assumed for damages resulting from the use of the information herein.

ISBN 0-7938-0355-1

www.tfh.com

Contents

Few fishes have ever equaled the classic beauty of a well-kept discus—or the aura of difficulty that surrounds the fish.

Starting With Discus

It is the purpose of this book to prepare the aquarist to keep discus successfully. Learning about where discus originate in nature is essential to understanding why the discus has certain requirements for its care in the aquarium. If these few basic requirements are respected, given that you have started with healthy fish, there is no reason why everyone cannot enjoy and keep these exceptional fishes.

WHAT IS A DISCUS?

A discus is a cichlid. Cichlids belong to a large family, Cichlidae, of many different fishes that share common ancestors and features of their structure. Some familiar examples of cichlids are angelfishes, oscars, convict cichlids, dwarf cichlids, and African cichlids. All these, and many more, are relatives of the genus *Symphysodon*, to which the different species and forms of discus belong.

Cichlids are highly esteemed fishes. They enjoy this status for many reasons, but the most important in hobbyist terms are their intelligence and distinctive spawning behaviors. Cichlids are the "personality fish" of the hobby, interacting in unusual ways with their keepers, each other, and their offspring.

WHERE DO YOU FIND DISCUS?

Discus are found on only one continent, South America. They are Amazonian fishes inhabiting the quiet blackwater rainforest tributaries of the Amazon River, the second longest river in the world. There they keep close to the shoreline where the water is still. They hide among tangled roots and branches where they are relatively safe from predators and maintain distinct territories that they would never leave were it not for the fact that the annual rainy season floods their habitat and shifts them about a bit. Otherwise, the discus would probably never venture more than a few yards from home in their entire lives. Discus are found in several countries, including Peru, Colombia, Venezuela, and throughout the length of the Amazon to near its mouth in Brazil. They are found in small streams, rivers, and lakes, but never in the Amazon itself. They always live where there is protection and the water is still or slow-moving. The water where they are found is very clean, warm, and has similar chemical properties throughout their range.

Outside of the Amazon region, discus are probably available in your own neighborhood pet shop. They are popular worldwide. Many pet shops carry different varieties of discus. They are also widely available through mail order from discus specialists and private breeders. Don't be in a hurry to choose; once you start looking for discus you will be surprised by how plentiful and attractively priced they can be. You will find advertisements for quality young discus in *Tropical Fish Hobbyist* magazine and discus specialty publications.

TYPES OF DISCUS

Discus have been known since early in the 19th century, when they were described by Dr. Johann Jacob Heckel. In the 1930s discus entered the aquarium hobby, where they were found to be very difficult to keep, impossible to breed, and extremely expensive. This made the "pompadour fish," as discus were commonly known at that time, all the more popular, as aquarists are generally people who are intrigued by the challenge of keeping and breeding difficult fishes. Well, it turned out that discus are not really that difficult at all, but they are specific in their keeping requirements. Once the aquarists "cracked the code," the discus hobby took off like wildfire.

WILD-TYPE DISCUS

Hobby discus can be divided into two types. There are the wild-type discus and tank-bred varieties, often (but incorrectly) called hybrids. Sometimes the wild-type fish are also wild-caught, but occasionally they are the offspring of pure wild stock that have not been crossed with other types of discus.

There are currently two species of wild discus recognized by most aquarists: *Symphysodon discus* (Heckel discus), with the subspecies *d. discus* (Heckel discus) and *d. willischwartzi* (pineapple discus); and *Symphysodon aequifasciatus* (common discus), with the poorly defined subspecies *a. aequifasciatus* (green discus), *a. haraldi* (blue discus), and *a. axelrodi* (brown discus). Many people are confused about wild discus identification because the colors of discus vary so

A typical common discus, *Symphysodon aequifasciatus*, showing the evenly spaced dark vertical bars on the body typical of this species in the wild. Breeders try to remove these bars through selective breeding, and many man-made strains lack bars.

In the Heckel discus, *Symphysodon discus*, only the dark bars at the eye, midbody, and base of the tail are prominent, the other bars being weak or absent.

much based on their collecting locality. Some factions would like to lump all the discus together; some people believe that there may even be more species of discus than we ever suspected! There are very few consistent differences between the two species of discus. In addition to some small differences in scale counts, the Heckel discus has reduced vertical banding except for the wide, nearly black vertical bands through the eye, at midbody, and at the tail base, compared to at least five or six (up to nine) evenly spaced narrow vertical bands in common discus. The wide black bands of the Heckel discus often are called the "Heckel bars."

Based on the thousands of specimens and photos I have examined and the reports of discus collectors, the discus can be said to be a fish that is relatively large, between 6 and 10-plus inches long, nearly round in shape, and laterally compressed (flat from side to side. Within the discus (which we will continue to treat as two full species), there is a great variety in shades of color, pattern, and body type. The coloration of the subspecies of common discus (*Symphysodon aequifasciatus*) varies greatly with locality and may not be all under genetic control. Some scientists doubt that the subspecies should be recognized at all, but instead that many local variations could be distinguished and recognized by common names. Many times I have been at a loss as to whether a fish was a dominant brown discus or a submissive blue discus. It's not so simple, and for our purposes in learning how to care for discus, not really important. What is important is that the Heckel discus is a bit more delicate than the other wild discus and that wild discus require a bit more care before they settle down in your tanks than do tank-bred discus.

MAN-MADE VARIETIES

Man-made varieties of discus (often called hybrid discus by breeders) are those that have been selectively bred for color, shape, size, or any combination of the three. Discus are quite willing to crossbreed with other types of discus, and this has enabled breeders to create strains that have never been seen in the wild. The discus of brilliant colors and large sizes that are available on the commercial market are not found in nature and could not survive there. In nature, the small, somewhat subdued fish is the one that survives. A giant brilliant turquoise discus would be piranha bait in short order, so it is only under the protected conditions of the aquarium that we can express the diversity that is hidden in the genes of the discus.

Some of the varieties that have been produced by selective breeding are quite remarkable. The high-finned forms, for instance, are majestic. Some people don't like unnatural

Though some scientists recognize several subspecies of both discus species, hobbyists should be more concerned with the appearance of the individual fish than wasting time trying to identify phantom subspecies. This young discus has some excellent golden tints.

varieties of fishes and are very huffy about man-made varieties in general. The simple fact is that breeders couldn't develop these forms if the genetic material didn't already exist in the fish. In my opinion there is nothing wrong with letting us see just what the discus can do!

The breeder's dream of a solid red discus, for instance, is close to reality today. Every month, advertisements appear showing photos of redder and redder discus. Not so many years ago the first strains of strongly blue-colored discus were just being developed. It was the dream then to breed a solid blue fish. This now has come to pass, and there are outstanding solid blue fish available virtually everywhere.

Varieties and Strains

There are many varieties of discus. Selection among the varieties is based on your own preferences with regard to color, shape, and size, but some varieties are hardier than others. There is sometimes a loss of vigor in the man-made varieties, and this continues to be a concern among breeders. Since the technique for "setting a strain" involves a certain amount of inbreeding over several generations, the quality of the offspring will deteriorate over time if some new blood is not introduced. Experienced breeders are aware of this problem and deliberately use wild fish or F_1 (first generation) fish to revitalize their bloodlines.

It is not unknown for some novice breeders to jump the gun a bit and announce prematurely that such-and-such a fish is a fixed strain. In their eagerness to create a name for themselves, they fail to plan for the large numbers of offspring that will not carry the desirable traits in the early generations of working with their crosses. Mating a pair of fish from two different bloodlines does not create a strain in the first, second, third, or maybe even the tenth generation. Given that discus do not breed until they are 9 to 18 months old, the creation of a new strain, a set strain, of discus involves a large investment in time, work, and space for raising.

Naming Fish

Discus breeding is not an absolute science. Even when you have the opportunity to acquire discus from a set strain, all the fish are not going to be of the same quality. Individuals vary in their color intensity, shape, and ultimate size.

Patronyms are often used to sell discus. Many breeders include their own names to sell their fish. This works well when the breeder has developed a solid reputation for the quality and the soundness of his fish. If you purchase a fish from, say, Bernd Degen, you can call it a Degen red scribbled. If you purchase a fish bred by John Doe, he cannot call it a Degen red scribbled, even if he has bred two fish he bought from Degen.

This brown discus displays excellent reddish colors with reduced stripes and bars, which is greatly desired by many breeders. With such an attractive fish it should be possible to selectively breed some very nice young.

He may only call it a red scribbled discus. There have been a lot of hard feelings over this practice, and you should be careful of instances where a person selling fish is calling the fish by a patronym not their own.

Green Discus

The most work that has been done to date with discus has been in the development of the turquoise strains. Originally developed from the green discus (S. a. aequifasciatus), the turquoise varies in intensity of color and barring. The color can be predominantly blue or predominantly green depending upon the bloodline of the fish. Some turquoise discus appear to have been crossed with blue discus (S. a. haraldi).

Wild green discus are often surprisingly bland looking when one considers that they are the broodstock from which some of the more extravagantly colored hybrids were developed. The background color of the wild green is brownish, yellow, or olive, and the horizontal stripes are a kind of metallic green, more like turquoise. In both the wild blue and green discus, there are occasionally specimens that have blue or green horizontal stripes over the entire body. These fish are called "royal" blues or greens and are in high demand. Some of the wild green discus, particularly from the Tefé region of Brazil, display blood red spots in the belly and tail areas. These fish are in high demand as well.

There are many good strains of turquoise discus, but the names can be confusing. Red turquoise, brilliant turquoise, giant turquoise, etc., are all names that apply to the turquoise strains. At best they describe the fish; at worst they are describing what the breeder wishes they were!

Brown Discus

Very few people are calling brown discus brown discus (*S. a. axelrodi*) anymore. It has been found that if you keep a brown discus under the proper conditions it may exhibit delightful shades of red, orange, and yellow, with varying amounts of blue around the head and in the dorsal and anal fins. For this reason varieties of the brown discus now carry names evocative of a fruit salad: cherry red, apple red, tomato red, tangerine, orange! These names are often accurately descriptive of the fish, but beware of young discus with intense coloration. It could just be that they have been fed a diet heavy in carotenes, one tricky way to enhance the appearance of the product. When a brownish fish is pumped up with carotenes (usually in the form of shrimp eggs), it will get very orange or very red. Unfortunately, this color enhance-ment is short-lived and you may end up with a very common mud-colored discus when special feeding stops. It may still be quite attractive, but you will never appreciate this fish if you feel that you were misled about its true appearance.

Blue Discus

The blue discus (*S. a. haraldi*) is very similar to the brown discus in most of its features, but it usually carries more blue horizontal stripes on the head and in the dorsal and ventral areas of the body. The face, as well, is generally a brighter color than that of the brown. There is said to be a difference in shape between the blue and the brown discus as well: The blue discus tends to be a little longer in the body and the brown is usually a rounder fish. Sometimes it is very difficult to distinguish between the two. Tank-bred blue discus varieties are often called cobalt, powder blue, royal blue (a misnomer in a varietal fish), or sky blue discus. These fish tend to be a strong, solid blue displaying varying degrees of iridescence and are often seen with blood red spots around the dorsal and anal fins and throughout the body. Solid-colored fish are generally very striking.

Heckel Discus

Heckels are real fancier's fish. Since Heckel discus are the most difficult of the discus to breed in the aquarium, they are likely to be wild-caught and thus dull in color, and they are not

Blue is one of the colors favored by discus breeders, who look for uniformity of coloration and also good body and fin shapes. This fish has interesting colors but is lacking in body shape and fin appearance.

likely to be appreciated by the new hobbyist. Heckels are very sensitive to less than ideal aquarium conditions and should be kept in somewhat warmer and more acidic water than common discus.

Many people are turned off by the "Heckel bars," the wide, intense black first, fifth, and ninth vertical bands that distinguish most Heckel discus from common discus. To an experienced discus enthusiast, the sight of Heckel discus in their full glory is an inspiration! The first thing the commercial discus breeder wishes to do, however, is to try to capture the lovely deep ground color of the Heckel and delete the bars! Many of the commercial varieties of discus, and not only the Heckels, have been bred specifically to show no dark bands or bars in the body. The state of the art in discus breeding is an exquisite solid blue fish that shows no markings at all on the body and possesses a blood-red eye.

All discus, regardless of colors, need similar conditions: warm, soft, acid water in a large, quiet tank. Keep things simple and your discus will respond.

Preparing for Discus

All too often we see a fish we must have, lay down our money, and hurry right home to put it into one of our tanks. This technique may work with some fishes, but for discus it can only end in disaster. Discus cannot simply be dumped into an existing community aquarium without a little ceremony at least! To keep discus well, you have to prepare yourself a little *before* you own one.

If you are reading this book before you have bought your first discus, bravo. I hope that the words I write now will help you to become an accomplished discus keeper in time, and you have made a wise decision to learn something about them first. As you continue in the discus hobby, I hope you will read many more books to make the art of discus keeping equally enjoyable for you and your fish.

Before we get into specifics, let's talk about quality. If you endeavor to use only choice aquatic products in your selection of aquarium equipment, test kits, foods, and medications, you will have much better results than if you try to cut corners in the wrong places. Try to use only the best products (not necessarily the most expensive), those that have a proven track record for quality. Discus are specialty fish. Treat them as well as possible.

WHICH COMES FIRST?

An aquarium seems to be the starting place in fish keeping, but let's not forget the stand. Make sure that your stand is well-constructed and able to carry the weight required. Most of the commercial units will have been crafted for the job and will fit perfectly under your aquarium. Many

Though discus often look best in nicely planted tanks, they breed better in nearly empty aquaria. Of course, there is nothing to say that a breeder can't keep an attractive display tank as well as business-like breeding tanks.

models are designed with storage space included, which is very helpful because fish keepers always need extra space to store supplies. If you keep those bottles and packages tidy and in one designated place, you will always be ready for emergencies. Wrought-iron stands are very strong and have the added advantage of being able to hold tanks on the top and the bottom shelf as well. This can be enough for a self-contained small-scale breeding setup. It's up to you what to use for a stand—you can use grandma's old, heavy dresser (if she'll let you) as a stand for a beautiful show aquarium, or those who are handy can build racks with 2 x 4 lum-

ber and angle irons. As long as the stand (and the floor beneath!) is strong enough to hold 8.3 pounds per gallon of water, the weight of the tank, gravel, and decorations, and the aquarist himself (as when you are leaning in to do cleaning), you can put your aquarium almost anywhere you like.

As far as the fish are concerned, adult discus are quite particular about the height of the aquarium. It seems that if they can't see your face, they don't know who you are and get very nervous. They do recognize and show preferences to different people. Vibrations are disturbing to fishes in general, and discus in particular.

A discus will only display good colors if the water conditions are correct. The subtle colors and patterns fade and the fins become ragged and unattractive when aquarium conditions are not the best.

Young seem to be less sensitive and are comfortable closer to the floor, but adult discus need to be at least 30 inches and preferably 36 inches from the floor. Additionally, being kept in tanks farther above the floor makes them nervous.

THE AQUARIUM

If you are an experienced aquarist reading this book to learn more about discus specifically, you know that fishes are most easily kept in a rectangular aquarium. The reasons for this are simple (including the greater surface area to volume increasing efficiency of oxygenation and releasing waste gases) and available in any basic tropical fish book. The same holds true for the discus aquarium, with one difference. Discus are very well suited to high "show tanks." Because of the shape and height of the adult discus, an 18-inch-high aquarium is the most comfortable.

Use the largest aquarium possible for your adult discus; 50 to 60 gallons is ideal for the discus show tank containing four adult specimens and borderline for six. An aquarium of this size may seem bare if you purchase six juveniles, but don't worry, they will grow better and more safely in this tank than if you were to start with a small tank and increase the tank size as the fish grow.

The exception to this, of course, would be if the six discus you buy are still very young. Those individuals under 3 inches (often called fry in discus terminology though really juveniles) should probably be housed in smaller tanks until they have attained some size. Small discus have a tendency to get "lost" when there are only a few of them in a big tank. They can't find their food quickly, and a lot of it goes to waste. The fish remain hungry and the lost food contributes to water quality problems. Avoid also the impulse to fill the tank with other kinds of fishes just so you can see some action at this point. As you will see later, including other fishes in the discus aquarium is something that must be done with knowledge and restraint.

Show Tanks

We will assume for the moment that you are keeping discus for pleasure. There are many people who have jumped into the discus hobby and right back out because their dreams about the profitability of discus breeding and the reality of keeping discus were light years apart. You must decide before you set up your tank which way you want to go. The techniques for keeping discus and the techniques for breeding discus are somewhat different.

The ideal tank, in my opinion, for keeping discus involves only aquatic plants, driftwood, gravel, and the fish themselves. There is really no better way to keep discus for pleasure. The natural habitat of the discus, while it is

These blue discus would make nice additions to any large display tank. Remember that fully adult discus may be well over 8 inches in diameter, so they can never be crammed into a small aquarium.

great for the fish, is not visually appealing in every sense. The creation of an artistic aquarium is not about exactly replicating the natural environment of the fish. Too often, we would find ourselves staring at a barren tank full of what looks like dirty water. However, it is not only acceptable, but desirable, to use natural elements in the discus aquarium. In nature we find very few plants where the discus live, but in the aquarium discus and plants complement each other wonderfully. The plants help to cleanse the water and the fish are comforted by the cover afforded by the plants. Small discus

peck at the microorganisms that develop on the leaves of the plants. It is also felt by some authors that plants have antiseptic qualities that help heal minor scrapes.

Breeding Tanks

One day you may find that the discus you have so carefully raised are starting to act peculiarly in a way not associated with illness! If you discover that you have a pair of fish and would like to see them mate and raise a family, you may want to set up a special breeding tank. Some breeders use 20-gallon high tanks for this purpose, but I find these to be a bit cramped. A 29-gallon high

These highly colored discus, showing the variety that can occur in closely related breeding strains, display best over a colorful gravel bottom that accentuates rather than distracts from their colors. Discus appreciate a substrate that prevents reflections from the glass bottom of the aquarium.

or bigger tank is really best. Breeding tanks are minimally furnished, usually with just a heater, thermometer, mature sponge filter, and a spawning surface. The spawning surface can be a piece of PVC pipe hung from the side of the tank, a vertical piece of slate, or one of the spawning cones that are sold especially for this purpose. Cleanliness is the order of the day, and the less equipment placed in the breeding tank, the cleaner you can keep the tank. You will be amazed at how much maintenance is involved in a tank that contains only two adult fish and perhaps a few hundred very tiny fry.

Growout Tanks

The growout tank falls somewhere between the show tank and the breeding tank. You may not wish to bother with live plants but don't want the extra work involved with keeping a bare-bottomed breeding tank. A growout tank is where a number of fish appropriate to the size of the tank are raised.

The ideal growout tank should have a gravel substrate, some driftwood, excellent filtration, and plastic plants (if you wish). The goal is to have a tank that is minimal work with the best water quality possible. Growout tanks are typically sized to the fish you are growing up. A 10-gallon tank may be too large for a spawn of week-old fry, but the following week they may be cramped in the same tank. Six months later, that same spawn may be bursting the seams of a 100-gallon tank.

NECESSITIES

When the aquarium is your pride and joy, aquascaping is a pleasure. A beautiful tank is a showpiece in any room of the house. Properly set up, this tank should require relatively little maintenance relative to the amount of enjoyment it gives every viewer.

Substrates

Use fine sand or gravel for the substrate. Quartz and washed river gravel are favorites. Discus like to blow into the substrate to find food. Covering the bottom of the tank is very comforting to them. In fact, bare-bottomed tanks must be covered from the outside, as the fish will become very disoriented if they can see through the bottom glass. Fine gravel is ideal for the plants as well. Make sure the substrate, any rock-work, and everything else you choose to put into the aquarium is chemically inert. Be particularly certain that substrate and rock-work will not leach calcium into the water, increasing its hardness and alkalinity. Some substrates that you would not want to use for a discus aquarium include crushed oyster shell and dolomite. In the rare instance that your water is too soft for discus, the use of these materials in a filter box may be appropriate, but they are definitely out of the question for use as the substrate.

If you are uncertain about the safety of the type of rock or gravel you want to use, here's a little test. Pour some vinegar on a sample. If it fizzes, don't use it in the discus aquarium. If it doesn't, rinse it off and carry on.

A one- to two-inch bed of substrate is adequate for plants and fish alike.

Rock-work

Rocks are best used sparingly in the discus show tank, if at all. They contribute very little to the tank and interfere with housekeeping. If you just like the look of a bit of rock-work, use it by all means, but be careful that you don't set it in the aquarium in such a way that food and feces can

Discus aquaria must be kept clean, so the more complicated they are, the harder they are to maintain. Heavily planted aquaria, though they show off discus perfectly, present their own problems, including both controlling plant growth and decomposition and more lighting than discus typically enjoy.

collect under or behind it. A piece of slate set in the tank on the vertical or obliquely is often a favorite spawning site in the discus community.

Backgrounds

A dark background will show your fish at their best. Black is very dramatic. Blues and reds are attractive at times, but discus seem to prefer green (personal observation). Blue discus in a tank with a blue background can clash. The same goes for red fish against a red background. Use a little imagination. Printed backgrounds can be distracting. Some people like to use natural substances like cork tiles for the background. I like to cover the back and the sides of the tank with heavy paper to give the fish a feeling of security. It is also possible to paint the outside of the glass with marine paint.

Driftwood

Driftwood is a big favorite with discus keepers. This is one accessory that really does remind your fish of home. Safe, natural driftwood is available at your pet shop. There are some very exotic-looking pieces but, especially for discus, be sure there are no pointed edges. When discus are frightened, they are *very* fast, and certainly don't look where they are going! In fact, most often when discus turn into "flying fish" it is a result of their bolting, reaching the tank wall, and going straight UP! It would be quite easy for a frightened discus to damage itself on a sharp point of wood.

Driftwood helps to soften the water as it adds tannins to the water. This is very much preferred by discus and one of the reasons, besides the fact that the discus's preferred "home" is among roots, that driftwood is a staple in the discus aquarium.

Heating

Discus require higher water temperatures than most freshwater fishes. Between 82°F and 86°F is comfortable for them. Temperatures below 82°F leave them vulnerable to parasitic infestations, while a temperature above 86°F is difficult to maintain unless you have an excellent heater. Temperatures above 86°F are usually reserved for their therapeutic effects.

The heater you choose for your discus aquarium must be of top quality because the high temperatures required by discus don't leave much room for error. Use one of the newer submersible heaters. I would prefer to see two heaters in any tank larger than 50 gallons. A 30-gallon discus tank is served well by a 150-watt heater. Less than this will not give you the ability to raise the temperature high enough in the winter if your fish need heat therapy in conjunction with certain medications. A 60-gallon tank is better served by two 150-watt heaters than by one 300-watt heater, and so on. Five watts per gallon of water will give you enough leeway to bring the water up to 90°F should it be required.

A good, reliable heater (or better yet, two) is essential to any discus tank. Submersible heaters give the best distribution of heat, but they are relatively expensive. Don't forget your thermometer!

Make sure that the underwater heater you choose is easy to adjust and that the temperature is easy to read. If you have difficulty adjusting the heater, you may delay making necessary adjustments beyond the margin of safety.

The thermometer you use must be accurate in the long-term. Don't skimp on this relatively inexpensive piece of equipment; we're keeping discus here, not feeder goldfish!

Warm water is very important to the health of your fish, but we don't want to cook them. You can determine if the thermometer is accurate at the time you buy it by comparing it with the other thermometers in the shop. You can also test a thermometer against a fever thermometer if you doubt its accuracy.

Lighting

Lights and tank covers usually go together. For the planted aquarium, you will want to purchase a tank cover that includes a reflector that can accommodate two fluorescent lamps. You can use incandescent lighting if you must, but remember that it runs hot and could overheat the tank. Most professionals use fluorescent lights routinely, and for good reason. Fluorescent lights are economical in their use and purchase, run cooler than incandescent bulbs, and will show the true colors of your fish. The right types of fluorescent bulbs are also ideal for your plants. For strong, healthy plants and the best color rendition of your fish, choose daylight or cool white fluorescent bulbs. If you have purchased a reflector with fittings for two lamps, you could use one daylight and one cool white lamp.

The reflector is a very important piece of equipment for the planted tank. A good reflector will maximize the amount of light that reaches the bottom of your aquarium where it will do the most good for your plants.

For deep, planted aquaria, especially when the aquarium is a showpiece, consider using metal halide or mercury vapor lights. These high-intensity lights burn very hot, so it is necessary

Discus often look their best against a simple and attractive background, such as blue paper outside the aquarium. Elegance often can be defined as simplicity in discus.

A large aquarium allows you to keep a nice group of discus. Medium and even large discus (if you can afford the space) look best in groups in simple aquaria with subdued lighting.

to suspend them some distance above the aquarium. They are, however, ideal for plant growth and will really spotlight your fish. Because the lights are raised above the aquarium, tank covers are not used with this type of lighting. Ideally, your plants will soon grow up and out of the top of the tank. Some will even flower if the conditions are right. The use of floating plants with this type of lighting will help to give the fish a break from the light when they need it. A good aquarium dealer will be able to give you complete instructions in the use and safety of high-intensity halide lights.

Tank Covers

Discus tanks are usually covered, particularly in the community setting. Breeders sometimes don't cover the tanks for efficiency's sake, but all too often they find that a favorite fish has taken a flying leap! A cover is not a luxury: Tank covers help to keep airborne pollutants from entering the water while they (hopefully) keep the fish in the tank. Evaporation is less of an issue when you use a tank cover, and it is easier to maintain even temperatures in the aquarium. Sometimes a simple sheet of acrylic is used instead of a manufactured tank cover; this can perform very well.

Tank covers, canopies, and hoods are now available in styles to complement every aquarium. Some very handsome models come as a matched set—canopy and tank stand.

Hybrid discus, the man-made varieties, often are more sensitive to differences of water quality than are wild discus. All discus need soft, acid water to thrive.

Water for Discus

Discus are not really difficult to keep as long as you give them what they want! What discus want is: excellent water quality, free of toxins like chlorine, ammonia, nitrites, phosphates, etc.; correct water chemistry, especially pH and water hardness; and proper temperatures, between 82° and 86°F. Excellent water quality is provided by your filtration system and water changing routine. Water chemistry should be periodically tested and determinations made for adjustments. The water should be soft, between 3 and 15°DH (degrees hardness), and the pH should be between 5.0 and 6.5. This is where most discus keepers have trouble. Discus would prefer not to compromise on these values. To believe that you can acclimate discus to harder water, to higher pH levels, or to lower temperatures is folly. The discus may live, may even breed, in such conditions, but they would be living and breeding under stress. In fishes, as in humans, stress shortens their lives and makes them more susceptible to diseases. Strive for the ideal rather than trying to cheat the system.

WATER CHEMISTRY

You can probably walk into any pet shop and find out what the general water conditions are in your area. That would be fine if you were trying to decide whether to keep guppies or angelfish in your community aquarium, but it will not do for discus. You will need to test your own water as it comes from the tap and continue to perform periodic tests to ensure that your aquarium water is up to par and within the proper range for a number of values.

Testing the Water

You should initially test your water for chloramines and chlorine, pH, and alkalinity. Once the levels of pH and alkalinity in your raw water have been established, you can decide how you want to handle the situation. Some raw water is just about perfect for discus with little or no modification. Some water needs extensive conditioning before the first fish can be introduced. Once you know these values, you may even decide you want to keep another kind of fish because it will be just too difficult, or virtually impossible, to modify the water to suit discus. After the initial battery of water chemistry tests, you should continue to test it for the factors mentioned, certainly after the first few water changes, and add a few more tests to the list: nitrites and nitrates, phosphates, and, in the planted tank, iron and carbonates. Simple, isn't it? Test kits have become very user-friendly in recent years. All these tests can be researched in a good chemistry book and the reagents assembled through chemistry supply outlets, but the test kits and electronic probes available for the aquarium hobby are generally inexpensive and easy to use.

Toxins in the Water Supply

The water company can be your friend or your foe. Chlorine and/or chloramines are routinely added to the water in many parts of the world. A simple color test kit will determine the presence and concentration of either. Removal of chlorine and chloramines is part of the process known as conditioning your water. There is more than one way to skin a cat, and there are many ways to condition your tap water. Conditioning is the process of adjusting the chemistry of the water to bring it into line with the requirements of the fishes you are keeping.

Chlorine is readily removed from tap water by activated carbon prefiltration, aging the water, or permitting contact of the water with the air through the use of a spray. Chlorine can also be removed by adding commercial chlorine removers. If you are conditioning your water with reverse osmosis or deionization filters, these processes remove virtually all toxins (and a lot of necessary elements as well, which must be replaced), but more about reverse osmosis and deionization later.

Chloramines are the result of combining chlorine and ammonia, which some water companies need to use for purification of the water supply. Chlorine is not good for fishes, and chloramines are worse. If your test reveals the presence of chloramines, be sure to use a water conditioner that is chloramine-specific. Aeration will not remove chloramines.

Water Hardness and Alkalinity

It may be that your water hardness and alkalinity are perfect for discus,

This pair of blue discus is being kept in a spartan tank before breeding. The water conditions in a breeding tank must be carefully watched, as there are no plants or sometimes even substrates to help moderate chlorine and other toxins.

but unfortunately this is not always the case. It is far easier to adjust hardness and alkalinity upward when keeping hard-water fishes, but lowering these values is by no means impossible, though it may be difficult. It simply involves another step in the water conditioning process.

Total hardness is the sum combination of the carbonate and noncarbonate hardnesses of your water. Total hardness is measured as °DH or ppm (parts per million). One °DH is equivalent to 17.9 ppm. How total hardness is expressed depends upon the author and his or her orientation. I prefer °DH simply because as a discus keeper, I like to see smaller numbers when I am measuring water hardness. If I were keeping African cichlids I might prefer to measure my water's hardness in ppm.

Total hardness is usually not a big issue in keeping discus; alkalinity or carbonate hardness is a far more important factor in the breeding of discus. This refers to the levels of carbonates of calcium and magnesium. It is measured in °KH or mg/L $CaCO_3$ or parts per million. One milligram per liter (mg/L) is the equivalent of one part per million.

Soft water is 3°DH and 0 to 50 mg/L $CaCO_3$; medium soft water is 3 to 6°DH and 50 to 100 mg/L $CaCO_3$; slightly hard water is 6 to 12°DH and 100 to 200 mg/L $CaCO_3$; moderately hard water is 12 to 18 °DH and 200 to 300 mg/L $CaCO_3$; hard water is over 18 °DH and over 300 mg/L $CaCO_3$.

The values for general hardness and alkalinity given above do not always match each other in any given aquarium being tested. It is entirely possible to have a higher reading of general hardness and a lower reading of alkalinity in a sample being tested. The lower reading for alkalinity is the more desirable for discus water. Discus will do quite well in slightly to moderately hard water. In fact, many breeders routinely keep their fish in these values to ensure proper development of the young, but for development of the eggs, soft to moderately soft water is critical. Therefore, it is not necessary to drastically adjust the general hardness or alkalinity when you first start to keep discus unless the values are very high.

Reducing Water Hardness

It is best to test the pH and alkalinity of your water before making any investments in reverse osmosis or deionization equipment. As long as the general hardness and alkalinity are in the ranges mentioned above, you should have no trouble. Driftwood and peat will both contribute to softening of the water. You may find that your slightly to moderately hard water will respond very nicely to the introduction of a piece of driftwood and a bag of peat in your filter.

Beyond this, or if you are at the stage where you are seriously considering breeding your discus, you can look into reverse osmosis (R/O) or deionization (DI) pretreatment of your water. Both of these methods remove all traces of water hardness and a very high percentage of the impurities in the water through the extremely fine straining action in the R/O filter and specific resins in the DI apparatus. Water that has been handled in this fashion is stripped of necessary trace elements and must be reconstituted before use in the aquarium. Reconstituting salts are available commercially. Some authorities recommend mixing the water with 5% tap water, but if your tap water contains toxins, this is not the best method by any means.

Household water softeners used in many homes are entirely *unsuitable* for preparing water for discus. The resins in these units exchange hardness ions for sodium ions, and additional sodium is contraindicated in keeping discus.

About pH

Discus are very particular about pH. Keep your pH below 7 and above 5.5. The ideal pH for discus is 6. At pH levels above 7, discus are stressed. Below 5.5, the pH is inclined to plunge rapidly, so I find 6 to be comfortable for both the fish and the fish keeper.

Alkalinity and pH are closely related. Hard water tends to be naturally alkaline. Soft water tends to be naturally acidic. This is because of the buffering capacity of the water. Buffering capacity represents the presence of alkalinity (carbonate hardness) and the ability of the water to maintain a high pH. It is a chemical balancing act. If just enough carbonate hardness is present, the pH remains at the desired level; too much carbonate hardness and the pH will remain high, too little carbonate hardness, and the pH will crash. Maintain your carbonate hardness at around 10° or 15°DH and you should have no problems with pH. Check your pH with every water change until you are able to get a feel for how your water behaves. If you notice that the pH drops quickly, you must replace some carbonate. If your pH resists change to lower values, you must remove carbonate.

There are many methods of lowering your pH, most with some form of phosphoric acid, from drops to powders, but one of the gentlest and safest methods is through the use of peat moss. Because the peat adsorbs carbonates and acidifies the water, you should be able to maintain desirable pH and carbonate levels through the use of peat alone.

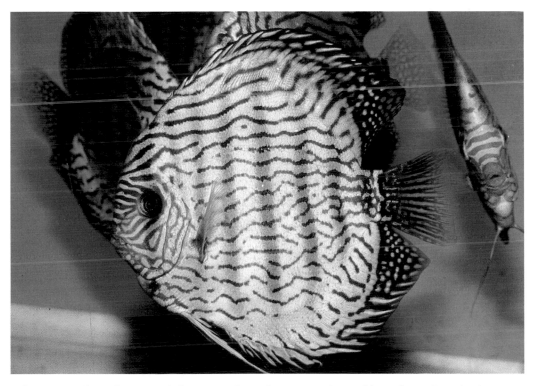

When several medium-sized discus are kept in an aquarium of less than gigantic size, you must make sure the water is always clean. Poor water will reduce growth rates and also damage the fins and often dull the colors.

FILTRATION

Filtration is essential. Filtration is the life support system of the aquarium. Without filtration, your fish would soon die from the toxicity of their own wastes.

The Nitrogen Cycle

In the aquarium, beneficial bacteria known as nitrobacteria colonize the biological filter media and every surface of the tank. *Nitrosomonas* sp. is the nitrobacterium that consumes the toxic ammonia that is produced by decomposition of fish waste and other organic matter. The ammonia is reduced to nitrites. The nitrites are consumed by *Nitrobacter* sp. and reduced to nitrates, the least toxic end-product of nitrification. This process is called the nitrogen cycle and is the backbone of biological filtration. The nitrates are removed from the aquarium by your partial water changes or in some cases by specific resins.

Mechanical Filtration

We should start with mechanical filtration. Sometimes this is called pre-filtration. The main goal here is to remove large floating particles of uneaten food, fish waste, and plant waste. There are many ways to accomplish this: sponges, pads, floss—practically any inert mesh-type material that will capture the dirt. Simple filter floss is very inexpensive and effective. Depending upon the style of filter you choose, the prefilter medium is situated where the water first enters the fil-

ter. It may be that you will be using a small sponge filter on the intake tube of your power or canister filter. Some filters have special chambers for pre-filtration media. Even the old-fashioned box filter with a layer of gravel and some filter floss will perform effective mechanical filtration. These fine materials trap the dirt as the water passes through them.

Mechanical filters *must* be changed or cleaned *weekly*. Most people do not realize that this is necessary. Mechanical filters capture the gross particulates, solid waste that must be broken down to liquid form before they can be converted by the nitrifying bacteria. It is far more practical to simply remove the solid waste than to wait for it to liquefy and then expect the biological filter to deal with its toxins. This is an error that very often leads to an overtaxed filtration system. Whichever method of mechanical filtration you choose, keep it clean! This is one area where you don't have to worry about preserving your bacterial bed. Just wash, rinse, or replace the mechanical filter media as often as possible.

Biological Filtration

Mechanical filtration is meant to take particles out of the water, nothing more. Usually mechanical filtration is confused with biological filtration because the same media are sometimes incorrectly used for both types of filtration. Biological filtration is the bac-

Filters need not be complex to keep the water clean in a discus aquarium. Remember that even with complicated filtering systems you still will have to manually clean the aquarium regularly and do partial water changes. Some filters give the aquarium a cluttered look, which is not a problem except in a display tank.

terial conversion of nitrogen-containing compounds as was described above in the discussion of the nitrogen cycle. While you want to clean your mechanical filter vigorously and often, the biological filter performs best when it can be left strictly to its own devices with a constant flow of particle-free, oxygenated water through the media.

There are many types of biological filters: the canister filter, which has been the mainstay of the advanced hobbyist; the trickle filter, which made its greatest impact in the saltwater hobby; the simple box filter, which is used with tremendous success by experienced fish keepers reluctant to give up on a filter that has been keeping fishes alive and well for the past fifty-odd years; the newcomer on the block, the fluidized bed bio-filter; and many more. Some tanks are maintained for years with nothing more than a simple sponge filter and air pump. The sponge filter is gently squeezed into a bucket of tank water once a week and the resident nitrobacteria do a fine job of converting the ammonia and nitrites to nitrates. Regular siphoning of uneaten food and fish waste goes a long way to helping you keep a healthy tank with a very simple filtration setup.

As many different types of biological filters as there are, there are more types of media. Some examples of biological filter media include plastic hair curlers, "bio-beads," gravel, sand, sintered glass, ceramic noodles, and so on. Biological filtration is critical to the health of your discus. Whichever media you employ to harbor your nitrifying bacteria, remember that you want to keep the bacteria safe from harm. It takes about six weeks for the nitrobacteria to establish themselves in the filter. During this critical period the ammonia and nitrite will reach high, maybe toxic, levels. Keep your fish load very low in the new aquarium and be very careful not to overfeed. It is suggested that the tank be run with one or two very small and inexpensive fish during this period. The water may cloud up for a period, a factor called the new tank syndrome. This is normal and will clear up presently. Once your filter bacteria have become established, the water will clear up spontaneously.

To maintain a healthy bacterial colony in the biological part of your filtration system, treat the media with gentle care. When cleaning the media, use only tank water. Do not use hot water or fresh tap water. A gentle rinse with tank water should be all you need if you have set up the system properly. The goal is to maintain the bacteria as undisturbed as possible on the media.

If your tank is without power for any length of time, it is entirely possible that your biological filter will crash. This happens when the bacteria are without oxygen for a period of time. This time period varies depending upon a number of factors, but should you find that the filter has been off for a day, smells foul, and the discus are gasping for air at the surface, do not simply turn the filter back on! The filter has become toxic and must be thoroughly cleaned and the media replaced before it can be used on the aquarium again.

Chemical Filtration

Some tanks do quite well without any type of chemical filtration. Frequent small water changes are employed to remove nitrates and other toxins. However, water chemistry varies radically in different areas and chemical filtration is sometimes necessary simply to keep the fish alive. If, for example, your tap water is very high in phosphates or nitrates, you may find that your discus don't do well until you pretreat the water with specific resins or activated carbon. While it is not within the scope of this book to go into great depth on water chemistry, be aware that there is virtually no water that cannot be made suitable to keep even such a delicate species as discus, if you wish to go to extremes in treatment. Water chemistry is a fascinating study, and in some areas it may be necessary to become quite adept at water chemistry and water treatment before you can keep discus successfully.

Activated Carbon

Activated carbon in granular or powdered form provides a type of physico-chemical filtration. Activated carbon removes discoloration, dyes, colors, phosphates, chlorine, chloramines, antimony, arsenic, chromium, hydrogen peroxide, potassium permanganate, some of the heavy metals, and many other toxins in varying degrees. It also removes many fish medications at the end of therapy. It is ideal for pre-filtration of the tap water to remove most of the residual toxins left after municipal water treatment and some of the toxins that have been added in water treatment. Activated carbon does not remove ammonia, nitrites, or nitrates, so do not expect it to take the place of biological or mechanical filtration. It does what it does, and it does it well and should be an integral part of your plan, but with full knowledge of its properties.

Activated carbon (AC) adsorbs the above-named toxins. Based on the concentration of toxins in the water, the effective life span of the carbon could be as little as a few hours or a few days.

Activated carbon is not meant to be used as a filter medium in biological filters. It is often combined with filter floss and left in the filter for an indeterminate period of time, but this is not the correct way to use carbon. Once it has been used to remove toxins from the water, it should not be left in the

The more crowded the tank, the more likely that you will need sophisticated filtering. Discus are large fish and produce quite a bit of waste, which can rapidly lead to a dangerously polluted tank that slows growth and dulls colors.

aquarium to serve as a biological medium. There are other, more appropriate media for this purpose.

Resins

Resins can be compared to magnets. The resin attracts a specific substance, like nitrates. The resin is usually placed in a canister filter. As the water passes through it, it "grabs" all the nitrate. There are many different types of resins that capture many substances. Resins have a limited holding capacity and must be recharged in a brine solution when saturated. There are different grades of resins, some having a long life while others are exhausted quickly.

There is no doubt that resins are highly effective and are used extensively in sophisticated filtration systems; however, if you use resin you must adhere to a regular schedule of water testing and maintenance.

Really, Really Fine Filters

Diatom and micron filters are used to capture super-fine particles of dirt. The material, either diatomaceous earth or man-made micron filter material, is so dense that even many free-swimming parasites cannot pass through it. The use of these materials for fine filtration is excellent for discus and their water.

Filter Flow Rate

For discus, you have to be a little careful. Some of the filters on the market utilize very high water flow rates. This is not good for discus. Remember that they need slow-moving water, hence a filter that turns over the water in the tank many times an hour is not a good thing.

Peat in the Aquarium

Peat, especially the types from Canada and northern Germany, has been an aquarist's helper for generations. Peat is an amazing substance in that it gives off valuable tannic, fulvic, and humic acids that reduce pH and acts as a natural ion exchanger and reduces carbonate hardness in the water. Peat will also bind up some of the heavy metals and other toxins that may be present in the water. The active compounds in peat are also present in the natural black waters of the discus. It is all-natural and does wonders in the discus aquarium. True peat filtration will color the water pale brown, but if the behavior of discus in peat-filtered water is any indication, discus really like amber-colored water! Peat filtration often triggers spawning in fish that have been flirting outrageously for months with no results.

Peat is available in aquarium shops and garden centers. It even comes in neat little pellets that are easy to use and economical. There really is no excuse for not using peat in the aquarium. Just be careful if you buy your peat from the garden center. Be sure that it does not have any additives that could harm your fish.

Peat is easy to use. Just pour about one quart of peat per 25 gallons of

In nature, discus are not typically found in crystal-clear water, instead preferring habitats stained brown by tannins and other decomposition products. To reproduce these conditions, some aquarists use blackwater extracts made from peat.

aquarium water into a nylon mesh bag or stocking and seal the bag. Slip this bag into your filter or place it in an area of the aquarium where water will flow through the bag. Replace the peat about every 30 days or when your pH tests start to show a rise in pH.

Blackwater Extracts

Blackwater extracts are produced by several aquarium manufacturers. Some are good and some are terrible. The quality of the blackwater extract depends upon the ingredients from which it was made.

Individual testing and constant water monitoring are essential when trying any new product in your aquarium because every aquarium is different. Try to find a product that is labeled peat extract, so you know that it is made from peat rather than old planks of wood! When you find a product that does not radically alter your water chemistry, stick with it and watch your fish. Their positive reaction, by spawning or becoming more brilliantly colored, will be your assurance that you have found the right blackwater extract.

Even a plain brown discus is an elegant fish when kept in a nice aquarium with the proper water conditions.

THE **GUIDE TO OWNING DISCUS**

Discus in Your Aquarium

It's finally time. You have set up your aquarium and the water is conditioned. It is time to bring your new discus home.

SELECTING DISCUS

How do you select a discus? Look for a fish that looks healthy first. A healthy discus looks bright and is alert and curious. Sometimes discus do not display well in a pet shop. The conditions may not be exactly to their liking or some naughty child may have been banging on the glass ten minutes before. The fish you are considering may be hiding behind the plants or the filter. This does not necessarily mean that they are unwell, but it could. Other signs to indicate that a fish is to be avoided are: short gill covers; emaciated-looking fish; darkened fish; fish with frayed fins or wounds; and fish with white, stringy feces hanging from the vent. The eyes should be clear and bright, the skin clear from defects, and both gills should be moving at about one beat per second. Breathing from one gill only is a sure sign of gill flukes. The fish should look well-fed. It's great if you can watch the fish feed. If they only pick at the food or take the food and spit it out, this could mean trouble. On the other hand, if they rush to the food and eat lustily, it's a safe bet that these fish are in good condition.

Be suspicious of small discus that show a lot of color. This means that the fish have been treated with hormones or fed color-enhancing food. A natural fish will not show much color at 2 inches. As the fish grows to adulthood, it gradually acquires its magnificent adult coloration; small fish, on the other hand, should not be bright blue, green, red, or orange! The eye, however, should always be bright and clear.

Some discus have red eyes, some amber, and some are not really colored much at all. Eye color is a personal preference. A gorgeous fish with an amber eye is not defective, but a totally black eye is a sign of ill health.

Ideally, you should purchase six to eight small discus of about quarter to half-dollar size. These are the sizes at which discus are most often sold. This will give you the opportunity to raise your own fish under your personal attention as to their care. Six to eight individuals is the number that makes them feel most secure and practically guarantees at least one pair when they reach sexual maturity.

ACCLIMATION

If these are your first discus, the community tank is the quarantine tank. If you are adding discus to an established population, you must keep the new fish in quarantine until their health status has been determined and any necessary treatment(s) carried out.

Ask the dealer about the water chemistry in the tank from which the fish come: find out about the pH, temperature, and possibly alkalinity. This is important because you don't want to shock your fish when you introduce them to their new home. If the water chemistry matches yours very closely, acclimating the fish to the new tank is very simple. If there is a wide difference, you must gradually acclimate the fish to the new (and I certainly hope better) conditions. When you get home, transfer the fish and the shop water to a clean bucket. This means that the bucket has *never* been used for anything but fish! Add enough tank water so that the fish can just remain upright. Over the next hour, gradually add more water until the temperature and pH match that of the tank. Then you can safely transfer the new fish to the aquarium. Some people use a net, but experienced discus keepers will use their (clean) hands. With a little practice, a discus will lie down in your hand and is easily moved from bucket to tank. If this is your first time, use a net. Throw away the water in the bucket. Do not add shop water to your aquarium.

At last the discus are home. Turn off the tank lights and let them settle in. They may lie down on the bottom or bounce around the tank at first. This is normal. Really healthy young discus will soon begin to investigate their new surroundings. After they have settled in, you can begin to offer them small amounts of food. Frozen bloodworms rinsed under hot water are nearly irresistible to discus and a great way to get them to begin feeding. Rinsed live adult brine shrimp are also taken with great enthusiasm. These foods are

Discus usually are offered at small sizes, which reduces the overhead of the breeder and also lets hobbyists buy the fish at comparatively low prices. These young might not show their full colors for months, but they require the best of keeping conditions during the time they are developing.

an important part of the discus diet. They may not be tops nutritionally, but they do keep your fish in very good spirits.

FEEDING YOUR DISCUS

Discus in the wild live on a diet of small insects, worms, insect larvae, and crustaceans. This means that they are carnivorous and need a meaty diet. Discus do not, however, need a diet of live foods exclusively. It is neither necessary nor desirable in the aquarium to duplicate the wild diet. Live foods often carry deadly parasites and diseases, so there are some live foods that should not be fed to discus except under special circumstances.

Small, frequent feedings are the goal of every professional fish keeper. While your fish may endure bouts of famine in the wild, we are striving to bring and to keep our fish in top condition at all times. If you feed one small meal of each of the following foods each day, you are almost guaranteed large, healthy, reproductively successful discus.

Prepared Foods

The quality flake and pelleted foods of today are specially prepared and highly nutritious. Several manufacturers have special lines of prepared foods specifically for discus. It is a good thing to offer these prepared foods for at least one meal a day. These foods have been enhanced with vitamins and mineral supplements, and while you may have to "train" adult discus to accept a new food, it is well worth the effort to do so to ensure that the fish are getting essential nutrients that may be missing from other, seemingly more palatable, foods that should be included in the diet.

We do not eat the same foods at every meal and neither should your fish. Offering a variety of foods ensures that your fish will not miss out on some critical nutritional element(s).

Live Foods

Discus love live foods. The thrill of the chase brings out the "wild thing" in your fish, and live foods are often used to condition any fish preparatory to breeding. Unfortunately, there are not too many live foods that are completely safe to feed. Brine shrimp, whiteworms, glassworms, and earthworms are about the only ones that can be used with any confidence. Brine shrimp are good for digestion but low in nutrients. Whiteworms are high in fat and should be fed sparingly. Glassworms are seasonal. As to earthworms, well, earthworms are fine any old time. You may want to keep earthworms overnight in a box with shredded newspaper to cleanse the earth from their digestive tracts. Then chop them to size and feed them to the fish.

Frozen Foods

Frozen bloodworms and other insect larvae, brine shrimp, and prepared heart and beef mixtures are major players in the discus diet. All these foods are usually accepted with great relish by discus of all ages, and there is a tendency for the discus keeper to rely heavily on these convenient foods.

Rinse frozen foods in a net under hot water. Frozen foods contain a lot of water, and they are none too clean at times.

Many people use beef, veal, turkey, and even deer heart as a base for frozen food mixtures. This food is very inexpensive, but it is labor-intensive as every trace of fat and tough sinew must be removed. The cleaned heart (or other *lean* meat) is finely ground in a food processor, other ingredients are added, and the mix is placed in small plastic bags in the freezer for storage. Other ingredients often include equal parts of shrimp, liver, white non-oily fish, cooked carrots, and a small amount of spinach. Unflavored gelatin may be used to hold the food together during feeding. This is a good food that is much enjoyed by discus, but it has a tendency to pollute the water very easily with tiny fragments of food and juices from the meat. If for no other reason, this food should be fed carefully and any excess siphoned from the tank within an hour after feeding.

Aquatic vitamins are added to the food after thawing and just before feeding. Be careful not to overdose the fish with vitamin supplements, but do use them. It is very difficult to ensure that all the foods you feed are nutritionally adequate, and the use of fish vitamins helps to avoid deficiency diseases.

COMPANIONS FOR DISCUS

Keeping other species of fishes with discus is a little risky. There are only a few kinds of fishes that can be kept successfully with them, and there are many people who believe that discus should be kept only with discus. For a planted show tank, however, the action and color of a school of cardinal tetras can really enhance the image.

Discus are very gentle for cichlids. They are easily intimidated. This is part of the reason that their tank-mates have to be selected with special care.

Another issue is disease transmission. Many fishes carry parasites without problems for their entire lives. These same parasites could be devastating to a discus in the aquarium. Because of this, it is critical that you quarantine and "debug" any fish that you want to introduce to your discus aquarium. Follow the guidelines in the chapter on discus health before introducing any new fishes, discus or otherwise, to your discus community.

The third factor involved is that there are few fishes that would be

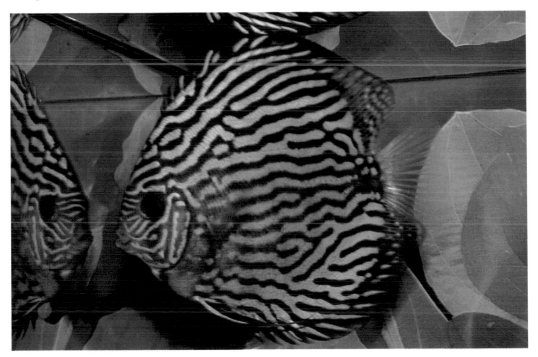

Discus love small live foods, but these are not always easy to get, so various prepared foods generally are fed to discus. Feeding crustaceans (shrimp, etc.) often increases red colors in discus.

comfortable in the conditions we maintain for discus. You have to find species that tolerate low pH, high temperatures, and low carbonate hardness. This more or less limits you to other species that are found in the same waters as the discus.

Some fishes that I could recommend as discus companions would be: cardinal, Congo, neon, penguin, emperor, glowlight, and lemon tetras; dwarf cichlids such as rams; and ancistrus, corydoras, and otocinclus catfishes. As for angelfish, include them only at the peril of your discus. Angelfish are much more aggressive than discus and tend to beat them into one corner of the tank. If you must keep angelfish with discus, place only very small angels with very large discus.

Do not, under any circumstances, attempt to keep plecos (plecostomus catfishes) with discus. The plecos will suck the slime coat right off the sides of the discus, and this will kill the discus. Also avoid any nocturnally active fishes. Their nighttime wanderings will prevent the discus from sleeping and disturb them greatly.

Do not forget to quarantine and treat all fishes that are to be included in the discus aquarium!

TANK MAINTENANCE

There is a considerable amount of necessary housekeeping involved with keeping discus. You must maintain the best water quality possible at all times if you wish to keep your fish in good health. It is often said that discus are prone to disease, but this is a bit unfair. When they are healthy from the start, kept in clean water of the proper chemistry and temperature, and fed properly, they are no more prone to illness than any other fish.

This said, let's see what we have to do to keep them well.

Discus thrive on clean water, but they don't appreciate large, intrusive water changes. To remove and replace 80% of the volume of the tank once a week will not make for happy discus. If possible, a drip system where the water is slowly returned to the tank over many hours is ideal. Lacking this, small, frequent water changes of 10 to 20% two or three times a week should keep your water quality very high. There are many variables involved here: fish load in the tank, feeding habits, incoming water quality, and the type of filtration you are using.

If you are using nothing but a sponge or box filter with floss and gravel, you will need to siphon frequently, not necessarily to remove ammonia and nitrites, but to remove detritus that consumes oxygen as it decays and will eventually produce a bacterial bloom. If you are using a mechanical filter that traps this detritus, cleaning this filter often will reduce the amount of water you must change. If you are using a mechanical filter, a biological filter, and a chemical filter with nitrate-specific

By keeping the discus aquarium simple, you reduce the need for maintenance, though you can never do without regular water changes. Most aquarists specializing in discus keep only a few complicated show tanks, instead preferring many simple, easy-to-clean aquaria for most of their stock.

resins, you will probably have to change relatively little water except when breeding your fish. With some of the sophisticated filtration systems available today, you practically wouldn't have to change water at all but for the need to maintain the proper level of trace elements in the system.

Testing your water for ammonia, nitrites, and nitrates will give you a good feel for how often and how much water you must change. Clarity is an issue for the viewer but is not always important to the fish. If you are using peat to condition your water, the water will be tinged a light tea color. The fish have no objection to this whatsoever, but some people don't like the look of the water. A little carbon filtration will remove the peat stain from the water, but not the beneficial effect of the peat filtration.

When changing water in the aquarium, make sure the replacement water is of similar temperature and pH as that in the tank. Rapid fluctuations of either will stress and sicken your fish. Ideally, your replacement water should be aged, warmed, acidified, and filtered through carbon before it is introduced to the tank. This will help prevent the fluctuations in water

Tears in fins may result from fights and accidents, but they also can be due to poor keeping conditions and even a poor diet. Minor fin tears that would go unnoticed in other fishes appear as major distractions on large discus.

quality that are so stressful to your fish. Many discus keepers use a 32-gallon plastic barrel to precondition their water for partial water changes. This is a good practice.

One important job that is often neglected is the cleaning of the inside glass of the aquarium. The slime that develops, often quite quickly, on the inside glass must be wiped away. It is quite sticky and a perfect breeding ground for bacteria. Wipe down the inside glass, especially the silicone connected joints, before every water change.

Use a special gravel-washing siphon to clean your gravel if you are using this for a substrate. You will be surprised at how well this cleans your gravel and how quickly you will remove the water from the aquarium.

PLANTS: REAL OR PLASTIC?

Plants can make a good aquarium a terrific aquarium or they can make a good aquarium a depressing mess. Aquarium plants have a set of needs of their own, and not all plants are

The gorgeous red spotting on these discus has been enhanced through selective breeding and also through proper diet. Red colors in discus often intensify when carotene is added to the diet in the form of shrimp and some plant products.

suitable for the warm, acidic water of the discus aquarium.

Some species of plants that do very well in the discus tank are: Java fern, Java moss, sword plants, species of *Vallisneria*, cryptocorynes, water sprite, and species of *Aponogeton*. By all means consult a book specifically about aquatic plants for important information on the proper care of aquarium plants. There are many advantages to including plants in the discus aquarium, but you will only realize these benefits if you take some simple steps to ensure that the plants you keep will be strong, healthy specimens.

On the other hand, there are many plastic plants that can be used to create an attractive display and provide shelter for the fish. Discus like to be able to get away from the limelight from time to time, and the use of driftwood and plants gives them the shelter they sometimes need. The more shelter they have available, the more confidence they will have overall and the more you will see them swimming in the open in full display with erect fins and bright eyes.

Algae

You don't want algae in any quantity in your discus aquarium. Algae are primitive plants that, while they won't hurt the discus, are a symptom of imbalance in the aquarium.

Brown algae are a symptom of low light in the aquarium. They are brown and dirty-looking and a sign of neglect. Wipe the brown algae from all aquarium surfaces and increase the duration and/or intensity of the lighting.

Growths of green algae, on the other hand, are caused by too much light and too many available nutrients in the water. Wipe the green algae from all surfaces of the aquarium, add more plants to compete for the available nutrients, and reduce

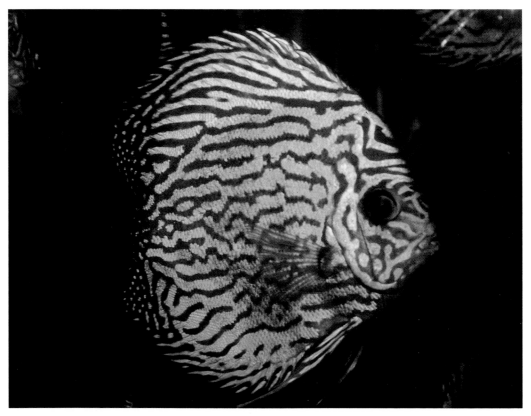

Bright lighting increases the chances of algae covering a tank, so the dim lighting of most discus aquaria actually helps control algal growth.

A discus will only show its best colors if it is kept in the proper tank, kept in clean water of the right temperature and chemistry, and fed on a diet that is at least adequate and preferably superior. Good discus do not raise themselves by just being thrown into a tank.

the number of hours you leave the light on in the aquarium to no more than 12 hours a day.

Blue-green algae are the bane of the aquarist and serve no useful purpose at all. Blue-green algae are the result of high levels of nitrates and/or phosphates in the water. If they become a real problem, you should consider using nitrate- and phosphate-removing resins, increase your water changes, and reduce the amount of uneaten food in the aquarium.

Wild-caught discus, even when colorful like this specimen, have been subjected to parasites of various types, often mediocre diets, and seasonally poor water conditions. That they remain healthy when transferred to the aquarium is an indication that discus really are very hardy fish.

Discus Health

I place this chapter before the breeding chapter because without good health your discus will not live long enough to spawn or simply will not be healthy enough to reproduce. While it is not the goal of every discus keeper to spawn their fish, to keep discus and never witness this beautiful sight would be frustrating in the extreme for most of us.

Prevention of disease is the best medicine a discus keeper has. Diagnoses are challenging for the layman (and sometimes even for the expert), and even a correct treatment is sometimes risky. It is far better to employ sound preventive practices than to helplessly watch your fish get progressively more ill as you try first one and then another medicine to treat a condition for which you are unable to pin down the cause.

QUARANTINE TANK

I cannot express strongly enough the need to quarantine and evaluate the condition of your newly acquired discus. It is the rule rather than the exception that discus are carrying one parasite or another when they come into a new environment. It sometimes seems as if the act of transporting discus alone is enough to trigger reproduction in parasites! Of the problems that discus develop, gill flukes are probably the most common and the least harmful to the adult fish. Jack Wattley, the world-renowned discus breeder and author, likens them to fleas on a dog, an aggravation to be sure, but not life-threatening.

You should have a quarantine tank up and running at all times when you are keeping discus. This tank should be about 20 gallons and contain nothing but a heater, a sponge filter, a box filter, and perhaps a plastic plant for shelter. The water should be of the correct temperature and chemistry for discus, well-aged, and ready for fish at any time. You will use this tank not only for your new fish but for any fishes in your community tank that appear unwell or are being harassed. With any luck at all, it may someday be your first breeding tank, but of course it would have to be sterilized before being put to this use.

In the meantime, however, every new fish you bring into your house, discus or tankmate for discus, goes straight into the quarantine tank for a period of at least four weeks. Make this an unbreakable rule!

MAJOR PROBLEMS
Gill and Body Flukes

Start with a formalin bath to eliminate any gill or body flukes that the fish is likely to be carrying. You know the fish has gill flukes if it is breathing out of one gill and pumping hard with that side. The other gill cover is usually clamped shut. Body flukes feed on the skin of the fish, and heavy infestations can be quite dangerous as there is a potential for bacterial infection.

Therapeutic baths should never be done in an aquarium. That clean bucket you have been using to fill the aquarium will do just fine. Twenty drops of formalin in two gallons of clean, aged quarantine tank water is

Any new addition to your discus stock must spend some time in a simple but adequate quarantine tank. This helps prevent the spread of parasites and diseases to your stock from an infected fish. Without a quarantine tank, you can never be sure that a simple trip to the pet shop could lead to the death of all your discus.

When kept in crowded conditions, as in a pet shop aquarium, discus often become stressed, which allows otherwise harmless parasites to increase in numbers and also in severity. Most wild discus carry parasites, but stress is the trigger that makes them dangerous.

used for a one-hour bath. Watch the fish closely during this time and be prepared to net them out if they seem distressed. You must use an airstone in the bucket. Formalin uses a lot of oxygen that is needed for the fish. If this therapy were performed in an aquarium, the results would be disastrous as the formalin would turn the entire tank cloudy with dead bacteria and cause it to become anaerobic. If you must use formalin in an aquarium, a much smaller dose of 2 to 3 drops per gallon is used with heavy aeration for 24 hours followed by a 50% water change and carbon filtration. Be sure you mix the formalin in water before adding it to the tank. Curious fish can

be severely burned if they swim into undiluted formalin.

Hexamita

Hexamita is an intestinal protozoan that causes severe intestinal damage. Discus that are infested with Hexamita usually face the back of the aquarium. When I first saw this condition, I thought my fish were deliberately ignoring me! The stringy white feces trailing behind a fish, sometimes quite long, are a fairly conclusive symptom of an Hexamita infestation. In severe cases, the fish become quite emaciated and the dorsal and anal fins erode into a scalloped shape. The fish usually turns dark; even the eyes darken. The fish approach the food and then turn away without eating it as if the thought of food sickens them.

The treatment for this disease is metronidazole and elevated temperatures. Dissolve 250 milligrams (mg) (1/4 tsp) per 20 gallons of water and turn the heat up to 88° or 90°F. Continue the therapy for six days, then perform a 50% water change; filter the water through carbon. You will see remarkable improvement in your fish after treatment with metronidazole. Coax the fish into eating again by lightly feeding frozen bloodworms or live brine shrimp.

Intestinal Nematodes

Capillaria, a roundworm or nematode, are present in the intestines of most fishes. It takes some pretty bad water conditions for these to become a problem, but we don't know what kind of trials our discus endured before they came to us. Fish infested with *Capillaria* are emaciated, with bulging stomachs, and tend to be shy. Treat *Capillaria* with flubendazole at the rate of a 1/4 tsp mixed into one ounce of food. Feed the medicated food once every other day for ten days.

Tapeworms

Droncit, or praziquantel, is the treatment of choice for tapeworms. Some fish have them and some don't. They are sometimes first seen as a rather large white worm floating in the water after being evacuated by the fish. Sprinkle the powder like salt on some food for one feeding, and in 24 hours you will surely know whether the fish are carrying tapeworms or not.

Intestinal parasites often are difficult to detect without veterinary help, but they generally are present in young discus. Such signs as extreme shyness and emaciation even when a good diet is available may indicate a worm problem.

Fungus often appears on the fins or even the body of a discus that is kept in a less than clean aquarium. The spores of saprolegnia fungus are always present in water, and they can grow in even a small cut or abrasion. Salt in the water usually controls simple fungus infections.

OTHER PROBLEMS

These therapies cover the "big four" fish diseases that are likely to cause problems in your discus. To be entirely sure about a diagnosis requires the services of a fish pathologist equipped with microscope and skill. The best the layman can hope for is that by quarantine and initial therapy we can prevent the spread of disease from new fish into our thriving and healthy discus community. Other diseases, such as fin rot, fungus, and bacterial infections, are preventable to a large degree through good aquarium husbandry.

Fin rot and bacterial infections usually respond to a nitrofurazone bath,

50 mg/gallon for four treatments, skipping a day between each dose. Change 25% of the aquarium water on the days you do not add the medication. On the eighth day, change 50% of the water and filter through carbon.

Fungus is quite serious, but again the threat of fungus can be minimized through good care. A wound that is attacked by fungus is soon deadly as the fungus eats into the body of the fish. Salt baths will take care of fungus quite well. Dissolve one tablespoon of non-iodized or kosher salt per gallon of water and leave the fish in the bath for three days.

Large orange ceramic cones often used when breeding discus, but any similar surface will do. Discus clean the area, lay their eggs, and then guard the nest until the fry disperse.

THE GUIDE TO OWNING DISCUS

Breeding Discus

To have raised a school of young discus to sexual maturity is an accomplishment in itself. To have them pair off, spawn, and raise their young must be considered a triumph and the pinnacle of the art of fish breeding. This is the reward for all your hard work and careful tending. The sight of a mated pair of discus courting, spawning, tenderly caring for the eggs, and then feeding the fry makes all the effort even more worthwhile. There is no way to adequately describe the magic of these events—you'll just have to make it happen in your own tank!

SEXING DISCUS

We can't. Don't bother your head about it. The fish know exactly who is male and who is female. To try to sex young discus is impossible. To try to sex adult discus without actually having seen them spawn and produce fertile eggs is questionable at best. No one, no matter how many fish they have raised, can infallibly sex discus. That said, I will tell you that the biggest fish is likely to be a male, especially if the dorsal and anal fins are slightly pointed. The female is likely to be smaller and with slightly rounder fins. That's about it, folks. Discus should be at least 6 inches in diameter to breed successfully.

MATED PAIRS

If way back when you were selecting your initial stock you purchased six juveniles of about the same age, you are well ahead of the game. Six to eight fish will give you an 88% chance of producing at least one pair. As your fish approach one year of age, you may start to notice that a couple of fish are spending a lot of time alone together, and woe to any fish that comes into their territory. This is a good sign that they have paired off and are in the process of becoming a real couple.

Another sign that this couple is getting ready to spawn is when they do the very graceful discus dance. The fish approach each other, bow, swim up, and circle back. There is a great deal of twitching and shaking, and the fins start to darken. As spawning time gets closer, the center of the body of both fish will become markedly darker as the skin slime starts to thicken preparatory to feeding the fry.

SPAWNING

Before spawning, and this may be days or weeks before, the couple will choose a vertical surface for their spawning site. This could be a cone, flower pot, the leaf of a plant, or even a heater cord. Lacking a proper laying site, in desperation some fish will spawn on the glass of the aquarium. Any spawning site is carefully cleaned by the fish pecking at invisible (to us) dirt on the surface.

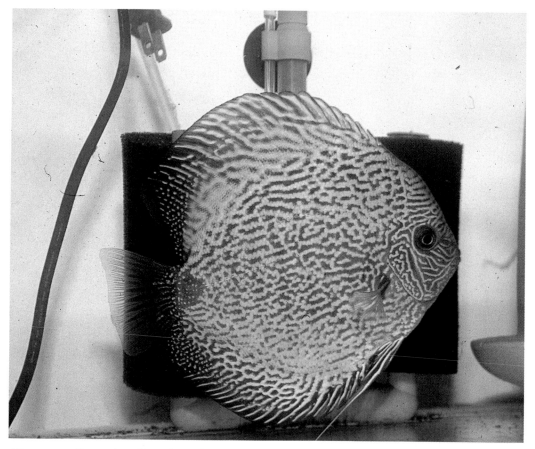

Discus usually are bred in relatively plain tanks, often without even a substrate. This allows the aquarist to keep an eye on the entire process and makes it easier to keep the tank clean. Fry react badly to dirty water, of course.

Because it is almost impossible to correctly sex discus without seeing them breed, hobby-ists and breeders put special value on proven breeding pairs. The only way to be sure of the sex of a discus is to see it lay eggs or fertilize the eggs.

If and when the time comes, the twitching, cleaning, and shimmying intensify until the female positions her vent against the spawning site and begins to lay her eggs. In a perfect world the male follows immediately behind and fertilizes each batch of eggs. In an imperfect world, he follows immediately behind and eats the eggs. This aberrant behavior is common among young, inexperienced discus and, unfortunately, also common in older, experienced discus.

Discus can lay anywhere up to 400 eggs at a time. The larger the female, the more eggs she can lay, so it behooves you to feed your fish well when they are young. Taking care of the eggs is a time of intense work for the prospective parents.

They constantly fan the eggs and worry about the spawn. Any disturbance at this time could result in them eating their eggs, so try not to disturb your fish unduly when they are guarding their eggs. If the eggs are viable, you will see the darkening embryo after about 24 hours. If the eggs are infertile, they will become white and probably be attacked by fungus about this time. The eggs that survive begin to hatch within about 60 hours of laying. After 60 hours, you will see the little tails wiggling wildly as the fry work to free their heads from the spawning surface, to which they are attached by sticky cement glands. As they free themselves, their attentive parents retrieve them with their mouths and spit them back into the nursery. Soon this constant retrieval becomes too much, and the parents move the fry to another secure place of their own choosing. At first you may think the spawn is lost, only to discover all the fry feeding from their parents' sides hours later. The discus parents have simply hidden their spawn in a dark corner for a time!

Discus and a few of their closest relatives produce a nutrient slime or mucus from glands in the skin of their sides. This is used as a food source by young discus for several days, while they are learning to feed on tiny crustaceans, worms, and insects. Though synthetic substitutes for this nutrient mucus have been designed by breeders, letting the young feed freely and naturally on the sides of their parents is still the best choice for the small breeder. It is strongly suspected that the mucus not only supplies nutrients but also passes immunity to common diseases from the parents to their young.

Once the fry have become free-swimming, they will move to their parents' sides to feed. Usually the parents take turns feeding the school and indicate that it is time to switch with a shake that sends the fry flying to the side of the other parent. The fry grow quickly on the rich "discus milk" that both parents secrete, and within a week they are ready to take newly hatched brine shrimp.

CONCLUSION

The above scenario is the ideal one. There are many slip-ups in this process and many, many eggs are laid that never hatch for one reason or another. Do not become discouraged when your fish fail repeatedly to produce fry that make it to maturity. This is a difficult task, and many times I have visited hatcheries where there were many adult fish but not a baby in sight! Politeness usually prevents my making much of this. It is far easier to raise discus than it is to breed discus. All the factors, known and unknown, testable and untestable, must be in balance before we can successfully spawn our discus and raise their fry to maturity. Good luck!